The Raccoon in Mushroom Forest

Chapter 5
Lesson 89: Special Vowel Sounds *OO* and *OO*
Lexile® Measure: 430L

ISBN 978-1-62382-044-2

Bruce and Gilda lived in a small cottage. It was just outside of Mushroom Forest. Bruce was a poor woodcutter. He made his living chopping down trees from the forest. He cut wood from trees into small logs. People used the logs in their fireplaces.

Each day Bruce and Gilda woke up to the sound of their rooster crowing. Gilda would cook Bruce's morning meal. Then she packed his lunch. Bruce would leave for work in his old, wooden cart. Then Gilda cleaned each room in the cottage. She was always in a good mood.

Each day Gilda made a pot of mushroom chowder for dinner. "How I wish we could eat something besides mushroom chowder," she would sigh. "Bruce works so hard. I wish I could cook him a better meal." One day Gilda said, "I will surprise Bruce. I will look in the forest for something else to eat."

Gilda put on her wool shawl with a hood. She went into the cool forest. She walked for a long time looking for something good to cook.

Suddenly, Gilda heard a sad cry. She heard loud whimpers, too. Gilda walked toward the sound. She saw a little raccoon. Its foot was in a trap. The raccoon was struggling to get away.

"Look at that," she said silently, "A fat raccoon! I can cook it for supper! No, I could not harm an animal. I must help it."

Gilda carefully crept up to the raccoon. She slid the trap off of its droopy foot. She scooped up the raccoon and put her wool shawl around it. Gilda took the raccoon home.

In the cottage, she cleaned its foot. She fed it some mushroom chowder. Then she made the raccoon a good bed by the fireplace. The raccoon snoozed. Gilda sat nearby and stitched up Bruce's pants. After a bit, the raccoon woke up. It stood up and shook its fur.

The raccoon said, "I thought I was doomed! I want to thank you for saving me. Your pot will always make whatever food you wish." Gilda could not believe her eyes or her ears. The raccoon winked at the pot on the stove. Then it waddled out of the house and into the forest.

Gilda ran to the pot. She looked inside. It was filled with thick, meaty chowder. On the table was a warm loaf of bread! She was so happy. She ran to the forest to tell Bruce about their good luck. "Hooray!" said Bruce. They never went without good food again.

The End

Comprehension Questions

1. This story is about a woman who goes into the forest to
    a. chase a butterfly.
    b. get some fresh air.
    c. look for something different to eat.

2. Gilda's husband is
    a. tall.
    b. dead.
    c. a woodcutter.

3. When is a bad time to *snooze*?
    a. when you are riding a bike
    b. when it is time to take a nap
    c. when you are lying on a comfortable couch

4. Why did Gilda creep up to the trapped raccoon?

    a. There was a lion nearby.

    b. She wanted to surprise the raccoon.

    c. She did not want the raccoon to get scared.

5. Gilda is

    a. lazy, but nice.

    b. mean and selfish.

    c. kind, cheerful, and caring.

Skill Words

cook	look*	snoozed
cool	mood	stood
doomed	mushroom	too*
droopy	raccoon	took
food*	room	wood
foot	rooster	woodcutter
good*	scooped	wooden
hood	shook	wool

Most Common Words

a	her	of	too*
about	him	off	trees
after	his	old	up
again	home	on	used
always	house	one	walked
an	how	out	want
and	I	people	was
animal	in	put	we
around	into	said	went
away	it	saw	will
by	just	she	with
can	little	small	work
could	lived	so	works
day	living	some	would
down	long	something	you
each	look*	sound	your
eyes	looking	tell	
food*	made	that	
for	make	the	
from	me	their	
get	must	then	
good*	never	thought	
he	no	time	
help	not	to	

Challenge Words

poor	believe	heard
toward	bread	

*both Skill Use and Most Common Word

15